Russia's Other Poets

Russia's Other Poets

selected and translated by
Keith Bosley

with
Dimitry Pospielovsky

and
Janis Sapiets

introduction by
Janis Sapiets

Longmans

LONGMANS, GREEN & CO. LTD.
London and Harlow
Associated companies, branches and representatives
throughout the world

SBN: 582 11746 1

First published 1968

Printed in Great Britain by
Cox & Wyman Ltd.
London, Reading and Fakenham

Contents

The titles of the poems are followed in most cases by the names of the clandestine magazines in which they were first published in the U.S.S.R.

Gleb Garbovsky

Viktor Golyavkin

N. Gorbanyevskaya

A. Ivanov

V. Kalugin

Ivan Kharabarov

Translator's Note

About one fifth of all the 'underground' verse printed in the pages of *Grani* is translated in this book. The quality of the material available is very uneven: the general policy has been simply to translate the poems which seemed worth translating. The translations were done from literal versions supplied by Dr Dimitry Pospielovsky and Mr Janis Sapiets.

Acknowledgments are due to Messrs Collins with The Harvill Press for permission to reproduce in translation the poem 'Hamlet' from Boris Pasternak's *Dr Zhivago*. My sincere thanks are due to Mr Michael Scammell, for many valuable suggestions; and to my wife.

K.B.

Introduction

During the past forty years, Soviet writers have been faced with a clearly defined choice: to conform, or to risk disgrace. Those who strike the right balance between their creative inclinations and the ideological criteria of the Party receive the *imprimatur*, see their works published, and are accepted by the Soviet establishment. Nonconformity invites censure or open disgrace in varying degrees: vilification, denial of publishing rights, court action, imprisonment, a term in a forced labour camp, or exile.

As a result of these ideological restrictions, Soviet readers are denied access to outstanding works which remain unpublished (Mikhail Bulgakov's *The Master and Margarita* and *A Theatrical Novel* appeared over 25 years after his death, the former only in a heavily edited version; Boris Pasternak's *Dr Zhivago* is still banned, so are works by Sinyavsky, Daniel, Solzhenitsyn and Dudintsev), while younger writers are cut off from contacts which would enable them to widen their horizons and to develop a more critical approach to their own work.

Especially remarkable for its viciousness was the period after 1946 when Zhdanov, Stalin's arbiter in cultural matters, made his scurrilous attack on Akhmatova and Zoshchenko: during the eight years 1946–53, Soviet literature virtually ceased to exist.

Stalin's death in 1953 came as a timely antidote to the numbness which had for so many years paralysed Soviet literature and art. Not that the Party's attitude had radically changed, but for a while it appeared uncertain of itself and relaxed its grip on Soviet public opinion. This hesitation was sufficient to bring about a significant change in the attitude of writers: after the terror of Zhdanovism, they now enjoyed comparative freedom and became conscious of their own power and responsibility. The process was slow at first: Ehrenburg's *The Thaw* (1954) was only a cautious hint of things to come, but Dudintsev's *Not by Bread Alone* (1956) with its merciless portrayal of Soviet bureaucracy and corruption in high places was a direct challenge to Socialist Realism and its easy utopianism. When the Party recovered from the confusion caused by the death of Stalin, it soon became obvious that the old discipline could not be reimposed. Many writers refused to be intimidated, and when denied publication at home they sent their works abroad, allowing them to be published in the West. Pasternak showed the way in 1957 with his *Dr Zhivago*. Besides introducing the young Russian writers to Western publishers, he restored to Russian literature depth, humility and a sense of the holy: love and religion, the two basic themes of *Dr Zhivago*, had been previously almost unknown in Soviet literature. Pasternak was the pioneer of the Russian literary revival and exercised a tremendous influence on his younger contemporaries.

In 1959 Sinyavsky (Tertz) urged in his essay on Socialist Realism that it should be replaced by 'a phantasmagoric art, with hypotheses instead of a purpose, an art in which the grotesque will replace realistic descriptions of ordinary life'. The absurd and the fantastic, wrote Sinyavsky, were the art forms which would best correspond to the spirit of our time.

Similarly, Daniel (Arzhak) in *This is Moscow Speaking* (published in English in 1962): 'I go along and say to myself: This is your world, your life, and you are a cell, a particle of it. You should not allow yourself to be intimidated. You should answer for yourself, and thereby answer for others.'

In May 1967 came Solzhenitsyn's indictment of Soviet censorship in his letter to the Soviet Writers' Congress. This was a remarkable document: 'Our writers are denied the right to express their judgments on the moral life of man and society, to illuminate in their own way the social problems or the profound historical experience of our country. . . . Editors refuse excellent manuscripts by young writers, still unknown to the public, for the sole reason that they "would not pass the censor". Many members of the Writers' Union, and even delegates at this Congress, know how they themselves had to submit to the pressures of the censorship and to give up elements essential to the structure and artistic design of their works. They have changed chapters, pages, paragraphs, phrases; they have sugared their writings simply to see them printed, and so they have spoiled them irremediably. The best of our literature is published in a mutilated form. . . . The redeeming moment is the death of an embarrassing writer: sooner or later, after it has happened, they give him back to us, carefully explaining his "errors". Not so long ago, Pasternak's name could not be mentioned in public, but now he is dead his books are published, and his verses are even recited on formal occasions. Thus Pushkin's words are truly fulfilled: "They can only love the dead." . . . The literature which is not as close to contemporary society as the air it breathes and cannot share with it all its pain and anxiety, which cannot in good time give a warning signal against moral and social dangers – such a literature is not worthy of its name . . . and is bought not for reading but for the practical use one can make of the paper.'

Meanwhile, the censorship is trying to reassert itself. *Dr Zhivago*, the stories of Sinyavsky, Daniel and Tarsis, and the latest works of Solzhenitsyn and Dudintsev, have not been published in the Soviet Union and remain out of the reach of the general public. Pasternak ended his days in official disgrace. Sinyavsky and Daniel were sentenced to detention in a labour camp, Tarsis, another rebel and author of *Ward 7*, was deprived of his citizenship while abroad, Solzhenitsyn – as he explained in his letter to the Writers' Union – has been suffering from relentless persecution, and Dudintsev's name has almost disappeared from print.

It is against this general background of ideological conflict that one must consider the development of modern Russian poetry. There is little doubt that poetry is even more vulnerable when imprisoned in an ideological strait-jacket than prose. A poet can speak only of his own experience of life, of himself – and when he is denied this, all that remains to him is silence. Thus we find that after Mayakovsky and Yesenin Russian poetry, in the true meaning of the word, virtually disappears from the scene. Apart from Pasternak and perhaps Nikolai Zabolotsky (sent to a concentration camp in 1937), one can mention Aleksandr Tvardovsky, Konstantin Simonov, Margarita Aligher, Olga Bergholz, and a few others, but it is only with Yevgeny Yevtushenko (b. 1933) that we are again in the presence of a poet in the brilliant tradition of the early twenties. This is a gap of some twenty-five or thirty years. Anna Akhmatova can hardly be mentioned in this context: she was silent between 1922 and 1940, became a victim of Zhdanov's abuse in 1946, and appeared in print only rarely between 1953 and her death in 1966. Her 'Poem without a Hero' and 'Requiem' have been published in full only in the West.

Yevtushenko's dynamic talent, reminiscent of Mayakovsky, his sense of vocation and frankness, have earned him immense success with young people. As Sinyavsky wrote about him in an essay published in the clandestine magazine *Phoenix 1966*, Yevtushenko has given back to his readers the lyrical hero, revealing in his poems the life and personality of the poet. It is from about 1956, when Yevtushenko published his *Zima Junction*, that poetry has once again acquired a dominant status in Soviet literature, with poetry readings being held all over the country before wildly enthusiastic audiences.

More recently, Yevtushenko's popularity has been equalled by that of his friend and contemporary Andrei Voznesensky (b .1933) whose acutely developed sense of form and language points to his kinship with Khlebnikov and Mayakovsky on the one hand, and with Tsvetayeva and Pasternak on the other.

Both Yevtushenko and Voznesensky have had disagreements with the Party authorities, but so far they have avoided an open clash. This may be due partly to their popularity and partly to the fact that they have always emphasised their loyalty to Communism, even though interpreting its philosophy in a somewhat unorthodox manner. Voznesensky once said that Communism, above all things, was characterised by the development of the individual personality. This almost reckless individualism came out strongly in the letter he wrote to *Pravda* in 1967, protesting at the circumstances surrounding the decision of the Writers' Union which forbade him to take part in a New York Arts Festival in June 1967: 'I am a Soviet writer, a human being made of flesh and not a puppet pulled by a string ... the important thing is not myself but the fate of Soviet literature, its honour, its standing in the world. How long are we going to continue pouring dirt over ourselves? How long will the Writers' Union go on using such methods? It seems obvious that the leadership of the Union does not consider writers to be human beings. .... Everywhere it's lies, lies, lies, boorishness and lies. I am ashamed to be in the same Union as such people.' One must be singularly sure of oneself to exhibit this kind of civic courage, and Voznesensky's letter seems to be a further instance of the growing self-confidence of writers.

Another young poet of promise is Bella Akhmadulina (b. 1937) whose philosophically orientated lyricism is highly subjective and unashamedly emotional. Her mastery of form is reminiscent of Gumilyov and the Acmeists, providing another link between past and present Russian poetry.

These three belong to a group of Soviet writers who want to find a place for themselves within the Soviet system while insisting on their right to remain individuals and not to accept any dictates from above. Many of them sincerely believe in Communism and maintain that rigid orthodoxy and obscurantism are a distortion of pure Communist ideas. They are, if one can use the expression, Communist liberals, and their sense of mission is so strong that they are prepared to defend their convictions even at the risk of an open conflict.

There is, however, another group of young poets who have rebelled not merely against misinterpretations of Communism but against Communist ideology itself, or even against modern society generally. Yury Galanskov (b. 1940) in his 'Manifesto of Man' calls for a complete rejection of the existing order:

Ministers, leaders, newspapers – don't trust them!
Get up, you on your knees!
Look – bulbs of atomic death
in the graves of the world's eye sockets.
Get up!
Get up!
Get up!
O scarlet blood of revolt!
Go and break up
the rotten prison of the state!

These radical nonconformists have little or no hope of publishing their works openly. This has led to the appearance of a number of clandestine or semi-clandestine publications which began to circulate in Moscow from about 1955 onwards. *Figleaf, Blue Button* and *Heresy* were students' magazines with few claims to literary merit, but they were the pioneers of a movement which has been steadily growing in depth and in outlook.

Clandestine magazines, anthologies and collections of verse appear in mimeographed, typewritten or manuscript form, and are passed from hand to hand among students and members of literary circles. These activities are probably carried out by several groups of students and young writers. The existence of one such group – the Berdyayev Circle – was reported from Leningrad in 1965, but the best known of them is SMOG, an organisation of young writers, poets, painters and sculptors (the initials have been interpreted as 'Word, Thought, Image, Depth' or, more ironically, as 'The Youngest Society of Geniuses'. On 20 June 1965, *Komsomolskaya Pravda* with lofty irony and condescension referred to the SMOG manifesto as a childish prank which did not deserve serious consideration. A few days later, on 27 June, *Pravda* published an abridged version of a speech made by the First Secretary of the Young Communists' League, Pavlov. 'A bunch of layabouts,' he said, 'have met somewhere and declared themselves ''the Youngest Society of Geniuses'', and the Western Press immediately begins to talk about the upheaval of a whole generation.'

That SMOG is not just 'a bunch of layabouts' is evident from the impressive list of its publications, some of which have reached the West. The magazine *Syntax* appeared in 1959 (its editor, A. Ginzburg, was sentenced to a two-year term in a labour camp), to be replaced by *Boomerang* in 1960 (once again the editor, V. Osipov, was imprisoned); these were followed by *Phoenix* (1961 and 1966), *Lamp, The Seasons, Workshop,* three books of poems by L. Gubanov, and several other publications.

The declared aim of SMOG is to bring about a revival of Russian literature and art: 'We are! we are, poets and artists writers and sculptors, regenerating and continuing the traditions of our immortal heritage' (SMOG Manifesto). The magazine *Sphinxes* (published by SMOG in 1965) opened with a defiant declaration: 'Let us not guess how long Russian art will be forced to develop under the prevailing abnormal conditions. One thing is certain: not for ever. Such is the logic of historical development. A nation cannot exist without art. . . . If political leaders have not enough intelligence to understand this, one can only feel sorry for them.'

The poems in this selection are drawn mainly from three of the clandestine magazines: *Syntax*, *Phoenix* and *Sphinxes*. They, and those which come from other sources, have all been published in the West in the Russian-language magazine *Grani*, published in Frankfurt-am-Main.

A few of the poets are quite well known both in Russia and in the West and have contributed their poems to official Soviet periodicals: Bella Akhmadulina, Pavel Antokol'sky, Bulat Okujava, Herman Plisetsky, David Samoilov, Boris Slutsky and Ivan Kharabarov; but the majority appear only on the pages of underground publications. Most of the contributors are probably students who belong to groups similar to those described by the Yugoslav writer Mihajlo Mihajlov in his *Moscow Summer 1964* (published in part in 1965 in Belgrade): 'In spite of constant threats of imprisonment in the so-called "labour colonies", students show little fear. They freely discuss and criticise almost everything.' Mihajlov had met admirers of Kafka and Nabokov, 'but while among the students of Moscow University, I never met a single supporter of dogmatic Socialist Realism'.

The emphasis in these clandestine magazines is on youth, on experiment, on attempts to break away from traditional themes and to find new means of expression. Cut off for so long from the mainstream of world literature, the young poets, naive and immature though they often are, seem to be groping for a firm foothold, trying to assert their individuality. Their poems are pointers to potential lines of development, indications of things to come. There is often freshness in them and directness of feeling which one would seek in vain in the works of most of the 'established' poets.

In spite of the diffuseness and the uneven quality of the poems, each magazine shows a distinct character of its own. The one unifying theme is protest, but it finds expression in a variety of ways: resignation, bitterness, emotional and political rebellion – a whole range of psychological experiences which reveal the irrepressible urge of the poets to find themselves, 'to be' – not 'to exist'.

Syntax (1959–60, edited by Aleksandr Ginzburg) is

probably the most pessimistic of these magazines. The mood is often one of resignation verging on despair:

When they call out
     'Man overboard!'
The ocean liner, big as a house
Suddenly stops
And the man
     is fished out with ropes.
But when
     a man's soul is overboard
When he is drowning
     in horror
     and despair
Then even his own house
Does not stop
     but sails on.

                    (Sergei Chudakov)

The authors of *Syntax* refuse to accept reality, but their disillusionment with life offers no answer. It is an honest confession of helplessness, almost a lament:

The whole world's lost in a maze
Of anguished obscurity.

No one knows what's to come
The answer's not to be found.

                    (Ivan Kharabarov)

One of the most promising of the *Syntax* poets is Iosif Brodsky (b. 1940) whose attitude to life is one of tragic irony and stoic resignation – typical of this group:

The world will stay false.
The world will stay eternal
maybe within reach of the mind
but still without end.
Meaning that faith in self and God
will be in vain.

Brodsky's brooding attitude is in line with his own fate: in 1964, the poet was sentenced to a five-year term in a forced labour camp for 'parasitism'. His trial, a depressing instance of modern obscurantism, aroused considerable interest in the West, and Brodsky became another Russian writer to be better known abroad than in his own country: a volume of his verse (translated into English by Nicholas Bethell) was published in England in 1967.

The world of _Phoenix 1961_ reflects a more purposeful mood. The protest is still there, but it has acquired incisiveness. This is no longer a lament or ironical resignation but a call to rebellion – as proclaimed by Galanskov in 'Manifesto of Man'. Not a rebellion by force of arms – 'For poets there is no such folly Before an enemy so strong', points out N. Nor (To My Friends) – but a challenge thrown out in the name of ideas:

No, ours is not to shoot – we know it!
But in response to real alarms
The period creates the poet
  And he creates the man-at-arms.

Accordingly, _Phoenix_ presents a wide spectrum of ideas and creative experiments. It is the record of a search for new, untapped worlds and new, subjective ways of expressing them, but there are many links between the _Phoenix_ poets and the masters of a few decades ago. It is easy to notice the influence of Mayakovsky, Pasternak, Blok, Gumilyov and many others whose heritage is clearly the foundation for this new revival of Russian poetry.

Among the 'Phoenix' poets, one of the most interesting discoveries is N. Gorbanyevskaya. Her unexpected images and command of language give a strange fascination to her philosophical poems and deceptively simple lyrics.

For Gorbanyevskaya, Galanskov and Yury Stefanov, the central problem is the relationship between the individual and the world, or the state: in other words, themes of universal application. A. Onyezhskaya's 'Moscow Gold' is a bitter attack on the Soviet system:

Golden the five year plan
And even teeth wear crowns –
Everything's lovely in
My fatherland built on bones.

Phoenix 1961 comes closer to suggesting answers to some of the questions which, as yet, cannot be openly discussed in Soviet literature. If the authors have not quite succeeded, it is largely because they cannot rise above the level of political polemic – the immediate present holds them enslaved, and the great themes and ideas are often submerged under a welter of tragic exclamations and critical denunciations.

Chronologically, the next magazine is *Sphinxes* (1965, edited by Valery Tarsis). Here the mood has again changed. The dominating themes are religion and national consciousness. The cover gives 'Russia' as the country of publication, Leningrad is referred to as Petrograd. Aleksandr Vasyutkov draws, on a grand scale, a picture of Russia's historical destinies in 'The Tale of Bogolyubovo'; Yury Stefanov, in 'The Descent into Hell', mourning the fall of his people, invokes the names of the Russian saints and uses almost Biblical language:

My people, hear
the death knell ring:
to Herod
Russia sold her King.

There is political satire by Boris Slutsky ('In the state there is the law') and Aleksandr Galich ('Silence is Gold'); references to concentration camps by Artyomy Mikhailov ('If you've never been in a concentration camp') and scornful rejection of the October Revolution by Leonid Shkol'nik:

We're the egghead lads
Of no revolution.
We've knocked conscience
                    unconscious.

Generally, however, a more composed and contemplative mood has replaced the feverish tension of *Phoenix*. The Editor points out that the one common characteristic of all the contributors is their refusal to be fitted into the Procrustean bed of Socialist dogma. To this may be added a discernible note of optimism.

Phoenix 1966 (edited by Y. Galanskov) is the bulkiest of the clandestine magazines and also contains a number of prose essays and articles. The poems show a convergence of the lines indicated in *Sphinxes* and *Phoenix 1961*; but political issues still dominate, and tensions are even sharper:

In any soul there is a bright
                                country
Where there is peace
                    and coolness
                                in summer's heat
But not for me!
To me all life is war
Peace sets my teeth on edge!
                            (Aida Yaskolka)

Far from treating these activities as childish pranks, the Soviet authorities have turned on the young writers with a fury reminiscent of the worst days of Stalinism. Sinyavsky and Daniel were sentenced on 14 February 1966 to seven and five years' hard labour respectively. On 1 September 1967 Vladimir Bukovsky, a member of SMOG and allegedly one of the organisers of a demonstration in protest against the arrest of the producers of *Phoenix 1966* earlier in the year, was sentenced to three years' imprisonment. He had already spent two spells in a mental home – a familiar form of punishment – for protesting against the suppression of writers' freedom. His two companions, Yevgeny Kushev and Vadim Delaunay, were given conditional sentences. The editor of *Phoenix 1966*, Yury Galanskov, was arrested in January 1967 together with Aleksandr Dobrovol'sky (whose article on 'Relations between Science and Faith' had appeared in the magazine) and Vera Lashkova, who had helped with typing. They were brought to trial in January 1968 together with Aleksandr Ginzburg, the editor of *Syntax* in 1959–60, when he was arrested and sent to a labour camp for two years. In 1964, he was re-arrested for alleged literary contacts with Russian émigrés in the West, and released a year later after agreeing to sign an article in one of the Moscow papers denouncing the émigrés as Western spies. Ginzburg was arrested again in January 1967, on the charge of having compiled a four-hundred-page book of documents on the Sinyavsky and Daniel case.

Galanskov was sentenced to seven years' hard labour on charges of subversive activities and alleged connections with émigré agents, Ginzburg to five years, Dobrovol'sky – who pleaded guilty – to two years, and Vera Lashkova to one year. The illegalities committed by court officials, the lack of facilities granted to the defence, and the secrecy surrounding the trial, have been denounced since in numerous protests and petitions signed by many well-known Soviet writers and scientists. A manifesto signed by Larissa Daniel, the wife of Yuly Daniel, and by Pavel Litvinov, the grandson of a former Soviet Minister of Foreign Affairs, characterised the trial as a 'wild mockery', declaring that it was 'no better than the infamous trials of the 1930s which brought us so much shame and so much blood that we have still not recovered from them'.

Perhaps the most dignified defence of the young writers came from Konstantin Paustovsky in an article published in the November 1967 issue of the Soviet literary monthly *Novy Mir*, i.e. some time before the Ginzburg trial began. The experience of the past, wrote Paustovsky, 'obliges us to do all we can to help the writers whose talents have unfolded so brilliantly in recent years and whose gifts only now become manifest, and to spare them from those hindrances that did not elude us, writers of the old generation'.

Paustovsky's appeal went unheeded. Appeals by Galanskov and Ginzburg against their sentences were rejected by the Soviet High Court in May. Once again, the Phoenix had been consumed in ashes – until its next re-appearance.

JANIS SAPIETS   May 1968

Boris Pasternak

A Poem

The hum has died down. I
        have stepped on stage.
     Leaning by the door
I divine in the far
       echo what is
     to come in my time.

Upon me night is fixed
        through a thousand
     opera glasses.
If it be possible
       Abba, Father
     take away this cup.

I love your stubborn plan
       and I agree
     to act out this role.
But now another play
       is in progress:
     this once release me.

But the plot is settled:
       the road's end is
     unavoidable.
I am alone. All falls
       to pharisees.
     Life is no green field.

Zhivago's 'Hamlet'

Bella Akhmadulina

The God

Just because the girl Nastas'ya
ran out barefoot in the rain
to provide another's pleasure
vodka for the aged man

she deserved a lovely god
in a palace drenched with sun
elegant and just and good
in a robe of old gold spun.

But to him where drunkards snore
where all round is poverty
the two blackened icons bore
little similarity.

Just for this the chicory flowered
suddenly the pearls were splendid:
like a church choir then was heard
the plain name of the intended.

He appeared above the fencing
offered her a yellow medal:
this way he was quite convincing
as a god in youthful fettle.

And her heart sang holy holy
for the dulcet light divine
for the blue shirt, for the jolly
concertina, for the wine.

And he lifted off her muslin
kerchief and (deceitful beast)
setting all the hayloft rustling
crumpled up her feeble breast . . .

And Nastas'ya combed her hair
took the kerchief by its corners
and Nastas'ya in despair
sang with gestures like a mourner's:

'Oh, alas, you have undone me
you have wrought me many woes
Why oh why did you last Monday
offer me a white white rose!

Willow, willow, do not wither
wait, oh make me not bereft.
All my faith has gone – ah, whither?
Only this small cross is left.'

Through the sunlight laughed the rain
and the god laughed at the girl.
Nothing happened. All was vain.
And the god was not at all.

Sarah Bernhardt

Her tears affected none –
the tears she had not shed.
Against an ostrich fan
her pallid cheek she laid.

Admirers in the stalls
screwed up a handkerchief:
where crimson curtain palls
her hands brought white relief.

They knew how warm the jewel in
her imitation ring
camellia's endless cool in
her white hands wintering.

But how resigned and fleeting
the handkerchief slipped down
how calm the heart was beating
oblivious of the pain.

People forgave it as
the curtain fell afar:
pale yellow rose bouquets
were piled backstage for her.

Holding the roses, scarce
a petal could she see:
down her cheeks ran the tears
dry tears of mastery.

●

Click. The bullet was engaged.
The wild candle settled down.
Oh how sorely he had aged.
How long all this had gone on.

Frontiers of old age fell as
he remembered far off days –
his old regimental colours
all the glitter, all the noise.

Old age brings no happiness.
He trudged, trudged out yesterday
for a look at the first ice.
There he loitered, solitary.

Then he started off for home:
heavy footsteps slowed and slowed.
Suddenly in front of him
stood this woman – oh my God:

back it all came – long ago
thunderstorm and deep footprints
and her shoulderline cut low
trimmed with a white cambric flounce.

Why for her here in this spring
was that spring beyond recall?
Eyes so full of suffering
she stood simply by the wall.

4

So, the mortal shot will boom
rattling the vodka glasses
and his wife's big hand will slam
on the coffin when he passes.

Reading of it in the paper
up will come his shameless friend.
For the solace of the weeper
he will kiss the weeper's hand.

It will pour a drink for him
and his casual glance will range
round to where some medals gleam
on a cushion, dead and strange.

Fifteen Boys

Fifteen boys – maybe more
maybe less than fifteen
with frightened voices
said to me:
'Let's go to the cinema or the museum of fine arts.'
I answered them more or less as follows:
'I haven't got the time.'
Fifteen boys gave me snowdrops
fifteen boys with broken voices
said to me:
'I'll never stop loving you.'
I answered them more or less as follows:
'We'll see.'

Fifteen boys live quietly now.
They've done their hard duty
of snowdrops, despair and letters.
They've got girls –
some prettier than me
some less pretty.
Fifteen boys brashly, sometimes smugly
greet me when they meet me

greet in me when they meet me
their deliverance, normal sleep and food . . .

You're wasting your time, latest boy.
I'll put your snowdrops in a tumbler
and their sturdy stems will grow
silver bubbles . . .
But never mind, you'll stop loving me too
and after conquering yourself you'll talk down to me
as if you'd conquered me
and I'll walk on down the street, on down the street . . .

●

What makes me different
from the woman with flowers
the girl who laughs and wears
a ring she will resent ? –

Four papered walls where I
return to, feel at home in.
The woman with an ermine
looks away haughtily.

Poor her. She looks away.
What if I scare her off
when she leans out to puff
ash in the bronze ashtray ?

Lord, how I pity her
drooping shoulder, pale arm
and thin white neck so warm
beneath the coat of fur !

What if her lower lip curls
into loud, sudden grief
her hand hides in her sleeve
the floor bounces with pearls . . .

Pavel Antokol'sky

●

All we who in his name
Have won renown
And passed in peace the time
That now is gone

    All we, his fellows, who
    Kept silence while
    Out of our silence grew
    The greatest ill

Who of nights could not sleep
And locked our doors
When he from our own group
Made murderers

    We who dispensed sweet reason
    Bear the bloodshed
    Of jails, the trials for treason
    Upon our head.

Let our contemptuous
Sons cast the same
Stigma on each of us:
Ours is the shame.

    These truths need not be weighed
    In any balance.
    We hate him who has died
    Less than our silence.

1956

A celebrated poem voicing the reaction of many to Stalin's death

Aleksandr Aronov

●

I wouldn't go, man
Into that age
With no-man snowman
On the rampage.

He goes out walking
And scares the bears.
(When you're not looking
He's on all fours.)

Across the sky
Skates the star-dust
Falling to die
Yet fall
        it must.

Magnetic poles
Grope in the gloom.
A small ball rolls —
Earth is its name.

Ballad of Tramway Art

Somewhere in town
a trundling tram
slowed proudly down
ahead of time.

And a man's fingers
drew a face
on the tram window's
foggy glass.

(Now was she pretty
was she plain? —
but breath
took pity
on that pane.)

Things come, things go:
please tell me, what
O glass and snow
will be her lot?

What expert wants
to save her looks?
Museums
prints
or fine art books?

The eyes are calm –
look at those lines!
And in them
swim
doors
windows
signs . . .

Merry Tale

1. Somewhere on
   A high hill
   Live some men
   Pretty well:

   Wear two coats
   On their back.
   Milk the goats?
   They just suck

   Draining life
   To the dregs.
   Find a wife?
   . . .Won't show legs.

2. Comes to them
   Old 'un, frowns:
   'Now's the time
   To build towns.

By this here
Glacier
Put a stair-
case
And house.'

Well, OK.
A good cause.
Not (they say)
What it was.

Fell a tree
Build a flat
Factory
And all that.

Colonnade
Patio.
But the maid:
'No no no.'

3. Hm, that's grand.
See him bolt
Underground
In revolt

In exile
In prison.
Dark parcel
Red ribbon.

Knock knock knock.
Dry your tears.
Parcel, look.
In it: Cheers!

White, Negro –
Freedom, soul!
. . . But she: no
And that's all.

4. Dear oh dear.
   Bites his lip.
   'Comrades! sure
   Summat's up.

   Dashka won't.
   Of all girls
   Her tits point
   Like pencils

   And I've gone
   Quite berserk.
   Can't get on
   With my work.

   Just let me
   End it all.'
   They say: 'Be
   Sensible.

   Let's get up off our backs.
   Let's get down to brass tacks.

   Our turn, lads.
   Yours'll come.'
   'These three kids?'
   'She's their mum.'

   My oh my.
   Stop the rot.
   We'll get by
   Like as not.

   Life will be
   Great one day.
   She'll let me
   Have my way.

5. I've told all
   And it's true.
   That's their tale.
   How 'bout you?

Lines on Lands

Perhaps, however outlandish it sounds
There'll be this sort of assortment of lands:
the Land of Bassoonists
and the Land of Cartoonists
the Land of Fatmen
and the Land of Batmen
the Land of Lovers
the Land of Plumbers
and the little Republic of Jazz Drummers
the Land of Wits
and the Land of Twits.
You register –
             and it's clear what fits.

– Have you seen the papers? Look, the blighters!
Of all the tricky international situations:
The Land of Readers and the Land of Writers
Are breaking off diplomatic relations!

– It stirs the blood of all the dreamers!
There's been a flood
In the Land of Swimmers!

– They sit
they can't get papers
they fret away their lives
these travellers
from the Land of Creepers
to the Land of Executives.

– Hello, you're not a Mod?
– A Mod.
– We're fellow-countrymen! Good god!
Goodbye, ma
Goodbye, pa
I'm off
      travelling far
Away to the Land of Lie-Snug-Between:
The Land of the Girls of Sweet Seventeen . . .

Vladimir Batshev

●

We must start all over again:
glue the bits together
                    mould
the new from no chance clay
putting no trust in stock
recommendations
                    reactions
                              reviews . . .
And realise just
          WHO
                    we're being nice to.
Look, our work can't be made up
from prescriptions, like medicine.
Alleys today are longer
they're aping all the avenues . . .
Captain, put me down as
beaten.
I fell asleep at my post in December.
I'm tired . . .
          I'm fagged out.
Chop me off today
like a tuft of hair sticking out of my cap.
Enough.
          Close the empty almanac
with its faces
                    its phases
                              its forecasts . . .
Transfer me, captain
to the old job of poet.

To Karelana

Though no voice should call
hands are on the wall.

Lips are on one side
though no voice is heard.

Somehow I shall get
through to you – don't fret.

If no voice should call
I'll knock on the wall.

Sh! Do you hear my knock –
the key's in the lock.

I must leave you this
fall, octoberless.

Footsteps echo still.
If you can – farewell.

If you do get free
burn this poem for me.

5 March 1966
Lyefortovo Jail

●

The state has need of me:
they don't turn off the light
nor in the mirror-pane
put out the lamp at night.
Everything fools and foils . . .
Just what is there to tell?
Here only the walls cough –
the green throat of the cell.
Now, sleep that knows no bars
creeps up, sleep that deceives . . .
And like the guard's footsteps
a drip, drip on the eaves
and like applause the peep-
hole lid clicks on the door
and groans sound through damp walls . . .
There's nothing to hope for.
Beyond the wall – secrets.
The day comes hard and raw.
Beyond the wall – people.
Beyond the pane the thaw.
To wrench the skylight-collar:
O spring, what must I learn?

Lyefortovo has eyes —
those outer bars that burn.

6 March 1966
Lyefortovo Jail

I'm Like a Count (a jingle)

Put me to the test.
Write me letters? Don't.
In the 'Sailors Rest'
I sit like a count.

Like a count – MY TEA!
It comes without sugar.
No daydreams for me
I'm an earthy beggar.

Like a count – prince, duke
all live in these rooms . . .
Unshaven I walk
without legs or arms.

Like a count . . . No countess?
Steady on. We'll raise
our water decanters
for her soul's repose.

Countess, this oath take
of deliverance . . .
Hoarfrost freezes like
insulin in veins.

Let them punish me
as they would a pest.
I'm a count, you see
in the 'Sailors Rest'.

'Sailors Rest': slang name for a mental hospital in Moscow.
Insulin is used for sleep therapy

●

to L.V.

Once more the same old dream
comes and goes
            comes and goes . . .
You and I must become
one flesh from lips to toes.
You run
            call out: 'Keep calm!
You're always worrying!'
What goes on in the dream –
are you too suffering?
Listen! The guests have come.
Bring
            pity
                        on a tray.
Once more the same old dream
continues on its way.
Sticks flung against the rim
fly off – now spokes do so.
I've stolen your old dream
let it come
            let it go.
Old dream, why have you come?
I beg you, go away.
Just why do you, old dream
continue on your way?
Years will file into gloom
dimming mouth, eyes and nose.
Only the same old dream
comes and goes
            comes and goes . . .

May – June 1966
exile. Siberia

Dmitry Bobyshev

Yonder Were Houses

Yonder was a house
on the other
shore.
The soldiers had a smoke there.
Yonder was a house.
People lived in it.
The soldiers came after.
Before this.
In the morning, silence. By day
children sang.
The soldiers went down the road
saw the house.
They broke the legs of trees
had a job getting them alight.
They listened to one singing –
scars all over his body –
unwrapped their rations
rustled, guzzled.
They smoked. Then they
stamped out the fire
and went off.
And so the end.
Yonder was a house. Yonder
was
a
house.

Iosif Brodsky

- Syntax 3

A Jewish cemetery near Leningrad.
A crooked fence of rotten plywood.
Behind the crooked fence lie side by side
lawyers, merchants, musicians, revolutionaries.
For themselves they sang.
For themselves they saved.
For others they died.
But first they paid the taxes
      respected the law
and in this unavoidably material world
pored over the Talmud
     idealists to the end.

Perhaps they saw further.
Perhaps they believed blindly.
But they taught their sons to be patient
       and to endure.
They sowed no grain.
    They never sowed grain.
They just laid themselves down in the cold earth
        like seeds.
And fell asleep for ever.
Then they were covered over with earth
candles were lit
and on the Day of Remembrance
hungry old men with shrill voices
choking with cold
shouted about peace.

And they got it.
    In the form of material decay.
Remembering nothing.
Forgetting nothing.
Behind a crooked fence of wet plywood.
A couple of miles from the tram terminus.

●

For then my thoughts, from far where I abide,
Intend a zealous pilgrimage to thee
Shakespeare

Past arenas, sanctuaries
past smart cemeteries
past churches and bars
past big bazaars
past calm and gloom
past Mecca and Rome
in the sun's blue glow
across the earth
the pilgrims go.

They are lame, hunchbacked
hungry, ill clad.
Their eyes are full of sunset
their hearts are full of dawn.
Behind them deserts sing
lightnings flare
stars rise above them

and birds hoarsely screech to them
that the world will stay as it was.
Yes. Will stay as it was
with snow to blind
and dubiously kind.
The world will stay false.
The world will stay eternal

maybe within reach of the mind
but still without end.
Meaning that faith in self and God
will be in vain.
Meaning that the illusion and the road
are all that remain.
And there shall be sunsets over the earth.
And there shall be dawns over the earth . . .

Soldiers shall improve it.
Poets shall approve it.

Verses on Accepting the World

All this was, was.
All this burned us.
All this rained on us
struck us, shook us
took our strength
dragged us to the grave
set us on a plinth
then cast us down
then forgot us
then summoned us
to seek other truths
that we might be lost
in the scrub of ambitions
in the thicket of prostrations
associations, conceptions
and among mere emotions.

But we learned to fight.
But we learned to take heat
from the hidden sun
and to steer earthward
without pilot or chart
but, above all
not to repeat ourselves.

We like routine.
We like the dimple
on our momma's neck
and we like our flat
which is a bit small
for a temple dweller.
We like to let our hair down.
We like to nod in the wind.
We like the swish of cotton
and the roar of sunspots
and generally our planet
is like a recruit
sweating on a march.

●

To get there, not by tome
                                    or home
nor by a scheme for piping water
nor by the thunder's distant boom
nor by a holy cause for slaughter

nor by the party's stern decrees
nor by a different frame of mind
nor by a rusty blunderbuss
nor by the sacred tablets' grind

nor by the scars upon Christ's skin
nor by the cross
                            or sanctuary
nor even by an ancient shrine
nor even by a bird's high cry

but by Prometheus' flame
above Diogenes' staff
flickering in the storm
but never falling off!

Etude

I embrace these shoulders and I look
at what looms up beyond the back
I see the proffered chair grow pale
against the iridescent wall.
The light bulb with its keener glare
shows up the shabby furniture
and makes the corner couch aglow
its brown leather appearing yellow.
The table is empty, the floor flickers
the stove is dark, a landscape has
frozen in its dusty frame: it seems
only the dresser lives and dreams
and quickens my unmoving stare.
If here a ghost has ever been
then it has left this house and gone.

Monument to Pushkin

And Pushkin falls
onto the bluish
piercing snow
Eduard Bagritsky

. . . and the silence.
And not another word
and the echo.
And weariness as well.
. . . He concluded
his poems with blood.
They plopped
earthward.
Then they gazed long
and tenderly.
They felt odd, cold
strange.
Over them grey doctors and seconds
leaned without hope.
Over them twitching stars
sang
over them winds
stopped . . .

      . . . The empty boulevard.
And the snowstorm singing.
The empty boulevard.
And a poet's monument.

The empty boulevard.
And the snowstorm singing
and the head
drooping wearily.

. . . On such a night
tossing in bed
is more comfortable
     than standing
on pedestals.

Pushkin was killed in a duel

22

Fish in Winter

Fish live in winter.
Fish chew oxygen.
Fish swim in winter
their eyes brushing the ice.
To
      where it's deeper.
Where the sea is.
Fish.
     Fish.
          Fish.
Fish swim in winter.
Fish wish to surface.
Fish swim without light
under a wan
      wintry sun.
Fish swim from death
the way of all
     fish.
     Fish don't shed tears
     knocking their heads
          against the blocks
     in the cold water
     a fish's
     cold eyes
     freeze.
Fish
     are always glum
because they're
     dumb.
Poems about fish
     like fish
stick in the
throat.

Vladimir Burich

My Tale of Igor's Men

It's all happened before –
                    the raw wind
pulling at the veld
evenings on the Kayala
                    and the Sula
the squeal of carts
                    the camp fires till morning.
It's all happened before –
                    the yellow sunset
curdling the fields.
It's all happened before –
                    but there's no
                              speech

to give it
        voice
              in verse.
Eyes
    snarl up
in the maze of
            Slavonic
                    curlicues
the grief
      of eight centuries
is looking for different allegories.
Like a squirrel
            my thought darts
like a flock of birds in flight
like a wolf in the steppe.
                        Epic's
                              broad

canvas
      tugs.
No
    not in the historic scrap
stuffed in museum galleries
tears
      that fell
              at Putivl'

you even now
                mist up
                        the eyes.

The Tale of Igor's Men (*Slovo o polku Igorevye*) is a celebrated Old Russian text of the twelfth century telling of a lost battle. The lines in italics (translator's) recall the Preamble. Putivl' is where Igor's wife lamented the defeat

Little tin
of tooth
powder
how pure you are
        how chaste.
No
I can't . . .
Where's that old tube of toothpaste?

I look hard at this world
it all clears with the years.
Fewer
women
are good for motherhood.
And more and more
are good
for sisterhood.

You want instant happiness?
What have you built
baked
or burled?
You may even have shot someone in the back . . .
It's a lie
I didn't shoot!
They pushed.
I withstood.

I love all natural things:
bread of dough
house of wood.

Asphalt hasn't got me yet.

Sergei Chudakov

●

When they call out
     'Man overboard!'
The ocean liner, big as a house
Suddenly stops
And the man
     is fished out with ropes.
But when
     a man's soul is overboard
When he is drowning
     in horror
     and despair
Then even his own house
Does not stop
     but sails on.

Vladimir Erl'

●

deep in the palm a look
solicitously tender
but confined to the palm
like a bucket at the bottom of a well
like a man in the well of a yard
a small yard among tall houses
rising up
like the fingers of a hand
like the fingers of a hand
that is holding something
in the palm
like a dewdrop
must be a look

●

over the hill the sun's crown
with its rim
over a stump of moss the crown
thrust roots into the sky
the sun thrust into the sky
roots overgrown with moss
roots up into view
into you
thrust roots into you

●

to R.

A friendly splash . . . Yellow sands . . .
A golden day at dawn . . .
The waves babble, gambol
                            entice
into their embrace . . .
O, singingbirds
with the eyes of hungry lions.
Here they are –
                blue days.
Here they are –
                words.

Yury Galanskov

Manifesto of Man

1

Oftener and oftener at dead of night
I burst into tears.
No, not one crumb of the soul's wealth
can be communicated any more.
It's of no use to anyone:
in search of the Idiot
so much is spent in a day!
And after work men go
where there's money and whores.
So be it.
Over the avalanche of man
I'll pass, different, alone –
like a piece of ruby
shining through the ice.
Heaven!
I want to shine.
Over night's
black velvet gown let me
pour the diamonds of the soul.

2

Ministers, leaders, newspapers – don't trust them!
Get up, you on your knees!
Look – bulbs of atomic death
in the graves of the world's eye sockets.
Get up!
Get up!
Get up!
O scarlet blood of revolt!
Go and break up
the rotten prison of the state!
Go among the corpses of the frightened
to fetch for the hungry
the plum-black bombs
on the huge trays of city squares.

3

Where are they –
those who must
strangle the necks of guns

cut out the sores of war
with the sacred knife of rebellion?
Where are they?
Where are they?
Or are there none at all? –
Behold – their shades are fettered
to machines by a handful of coins.

4
Man has vanished.
Insignificant as a fly
he barely moves across the page.
I'll go out on the square
and into the city's ear
I'll hammer a cry of despair . . .
Then, drawing a gun
I'll press it hard against my temple . . .
I'll let no one trample
the soul's white relict.
People!
Leave off, there's no point . . .
Stop comforting me.
Anyway amid your hell
there's nothing left for me to breathe!
Greet Cowardice and Hunger!
And I, flat on my face
spit on your iron city
crammed with money and filth.

5
Heaven!
I don't know what I'm doing . . .
If I had a knife for vengeance!
Look, someone has poured
a black lie over the white.
Look
the evening gloom
chews the bloodstained banner . . .
And life is terrible as a prison
built on bones.

I'm falling!
I'm falling!
I'm falling!
I leave it to you to grow bald.
I shall not feed on carrion
like the rest:
I shall not stuff my guts
with fruit plucked out of graves.
I don't want your bread
kneaded with tears.
And I'm falling, and I'm soaring
half delirious
half asleep . . .
And I feel
man
blooming in me.

6
Here we're used to seeing
as they pass
through the streets in their time off
life-befouled faces
like yours.
And suddenly
like peals of thunder
like Christ's coming into the world
trampled and crucified
rose
the beauty of man.
This is me
calling to truth and revolt
willing no more to serve
I break your black tethers
woven of lies.
This is me
chained by the law
crying the manifesto of man!
And no matter that on my body's marble
the raven's beak should carve
a cross!

Aleksandr Galich

Friends go away

Sphinxes 1

Friends go away, away, away.
One into nowhere and one to be king.
In days of spring and in days of fall
As if the days were Sundays all.
Away, away, away
My friends, they go away.

Don't hurry to whisper 'they've gone' –
In your words I put no trust
But the newspaper comes at dawn
And the paper confirms they're lost.
Oh to know in time whom to shun
And to whom a smile was the Host.
Some leave on page twenty-one
But many more leave on the first.

Friends go away, away, away.
To one many torments, to one wandering.
Such a wind blows from year to year
It mows down the stranger nor spares the most dear.
Away, away, away
My friends, they go away.

We dreamed of a hill and a valley
We met on the isles of Hawaii
And I called in a wild reveille
The friends who had not gone to die.
By their touch, their weight, their odour
I inspect them, but by and by
The paper once more gives the order
To serve my time with a sigh.

Friends go away, away, away.
They go like a squadron at night thundering
Behind them the fields and the victory song
And only the camps to cheer them along.
Away, away, away
My friends, they go away.

Sometimes a crash, a disaster.
The whole planet is covered in blood.
Cold comfort that everyone's lost a
Loved one in this neighbourhood.
Don't offer me grief for the keeping
As though it were money or bread.
It's not for the dead that I'm weeping
I don't know who's living or dead.

Friends go away, away, away.
One into nowhere and one to be king.
In days of spring and in days of fall
As if the days were Sundays all.
Away, away, away
My friends, they go away.

Silence is Gold

We've been big boys for some while and
Put away childish things
And after Treasure Island
We don't long for diamond rings
Nor for the heat, the cold
Nor voyages God knows where
But seeing that silence is gold
You might say business is fair.

Mum's the word – and you'll get preferred.
Mum's the word, mum's the word, mum's the word.

And not trusting heart or mind
Choosing in all to ignore
How often we've gone dumb or blind
Not against, of course, but 'for'.
Where now are the pitiers, the pleaders?
They've vanished before they were old
And the silent are now the top bleeders
All because silence is gold.

Mum's the word – and you'll get preferred.
Mum's the word, mum's the word, mum's the word.

And now we're on top of the pile
The speeches torment us a lot.
Our pearls they may glitter – meanwhile
Our dumbness seeps through like a blot.
Let other men holler with woe
With pain or despair or with cold
Silence is sounder – *we* know
Just because silence is gold.

This is the way to get preferred
This is the way to become top turd
This is the way to give 'em the bird –
Mum's the word, mum's the word, mum's the word.

A Word in Jewish Ears

Ach Jews, don't stitch at tunics and trews:
You'll never be gentlemen's gentlemen, Jews.
Don't grumble – there's no future in it:
You'll never sit in Synod or Senate.
No, you shall sit in unholy places
And walk in shoes stripped of their laces
And not on the sabbath raise your glass
But before shrill tribunals pass.
Yet if you ply an oily trade
There's a good profit to be made
And they will call you faithful Dobbin
With medals on your cape a-bobbing.
This is the truth, the truth, I say –
Will be tomorrow what is today
And what's a forecast may soon be news
So Jews, don't stitch at tunics and trews.

Gleb Garbovsky

To the Nyeva

I may not come back to the Nyeva
                                a young man . . .
What then?
How behave then towards the Nyeva?
Will the girls
                like ice floes
sail past me
as if I'm not myself
indifferent to girls
                        to them . . .
I may not come back to the Nyeva a young man . . .
How then smile at her
                        with an old man's mouth?
With a rheumatic frame
                            how then without galoshes
without a padded
                    muffled overcoat
catch up with
                the youngsters in the fog?
, . . I'll come back to you
                            believing –
it's my lot
all this is my lot
in years to come . . .
I'll come back to you loving
                                nevertheless
even if I come back
                    to die . . .

The Donkey in the Nyevsky Prospekt

A circus donkey, ginger, rather small
right in the thick of Nyevsky traffic is
drawing a cart. Cut in the cart a hole:
BOX OFFICE Tickets – All Performances.

This donkey is ridiculously shy.
Even when children call he hardly cares.
The city – with the traffic roaring by
all round the donkey. He has baggy ears.

35

Shy little donkey . . .
Tugging at the heart.
The donkey is a slave, like me
                              of art.

After the War

First the bison lost their verve
languished in their small reserve.
Then the hippopotami
retched till it was time to die.
Scurvy took the mountain goat.
Flies were paralysed (but not
yet did they quietus find).
Now the porcupine declined:
he, though prickly still at first
soon went blunt, gave up the ghost.
Household pets went petrified
and the cancer virus died.
Death came finally to man . . .
Thick snow fell on hill and plain
glittering along the equator
blue upon the wide sea water
but no track of sledge appeared
and no skidding tyre was heard.
Over cars snow spread its cover
chimney-fingers stuck up black:
Earth was slowly growing slack
turning to a vast cadaver.
Past dead Earth's periphery
hurtling Marsward, astronauts
went on smoking cigarettes
sucking sweets for energy.
All contact with Earth was gone.
They sat stock still and silent.
Light bulbs on the instrument
panel flickered off and on . . .

The Perpetual Worker

thirstily slept
devouring sleep
bloodthirstily slept
as if he drank . . .
Often juddered
like a jeep
howled like a plane in a steep
dive. Sleep didn't come to him
he went to sleep
crawled on his belly
charged like a tank!
. . . To meet the morning
in full volley
even while he slept, kept
                              working.

Viktor Golyavkin

The Door

The wind whistled through the room as it would in a
  chimney.
This door had no hinges.
And it had no handle.
And it had no keyhole.
And it wasn't entirely a door.
And on the whole it entirely wasn't a door.
It rested on two chairs, and on it lay my dead father.

Banging Bellies

Eighty-five men banged bellies with such force that
thirty-five of them died on the spot. Then fifty men
banged bellies with such tremendous force that only
one survived. He ate a cucumber and went to the ends
of the earth to bang bellies with somebody else.

Aah . . . Aargh

A man died. They put him in a coffin. They wanted to
lower the coffin into the grave, but they couldn't
find a rope anywhere. Then they kicked the coffin
into the grave. The dead man leapt out of the coffin,
sat up and naïvely said:
– Aah . . . aargh . . .

Three Actors

One said five words: 'The gentlemen have been served.'
A second boomed right through the play in the leading role.
A third, in a crowd scene, shouted 'Hurray.'
The first got twenty roubles.
The second got about a thousand.
While the third got so little that he never shouted
hurray again.

N. Gorbanyevskaya

●   The fishermen cast the net . . .   Phoenix 1

The nets could not be fuller.
All around are the nets.
The sea wave's modish colour
In the dredged water sets.

The nets are swarming, flush
With poets. And the tails
Of every shade of fish
Twitch on the brimming pails.

The nets could not be fuller.
My friend, beware the threats.
Beware the sea wave's colour.
All around are the nets.

●

Oh, my friend!
I'm getting scared.
And I say: Oh, my friend! I'm bored.
And I say: Let's go, let's walk
down the street
where there are cars
and people
and where cars are cars
and people are people
and wet snow falls.

●

Once in Galicia (mighty land)
The realm of Yaroslav the Clever
A pail fell from a maiden's hand
And all the land was flooded over.

The waves of cavalry swept deeper
Through towns the fire in passion roared
Down bloody roads beyond the Dnieper
Went thundering the barbarian horde.

The aspens soon lost confidence
In the sweet apple of their eye . . .

Russian, Ruthenian ever since
Have skulls askance and eyes awry.

●

Phoenix 1966

In my own twentieth century
where death queues for a grave
my wretched passion, my
for ever lonely love

amid these Goya settings puts
up just as poor a show
as after screaming jets
the trump of Jericho.

●

In the asylum
shatter your palm
to the wall your brow
as your face to snow.

To violent darkness
with joyful face
headlong Russia goes
as into mirrors.

A dose for her son
of stelazine
and for his mother
a stygian soldier.

Stelazine: a powerful sedative used in the
treatment of schizophrenia

A. Ivanov

●

This evening when the pane
Is blind with Arctic weather
At table once again
We take our seats together.
Comrade, don't tell me lies
Of better things tomorrow:
The rings are round the eyes
In hearts alarm and sorrow.

●

White hill looms against the black
Eyebrows mourn against the brown.
Lips' red ribbons laugh and joke
But the eyes look down, look down.
You can't shackle, bind or truss
The last train, nor can you catch
The last hope of happiness
The last cigarette, last match.
'May I join you?' 'Do sit down.'
'May I look into your eyes?'
Silence. And a station ran
Past flinging dead leaves at us.

V. Kalugin

Creative Work

The Song about the Bird

A man caught a bird
a man caught a bird –
its like had never been seen before.
– I'll kill you, the man said.
The bird grew still more beautiful.
– I'll kill you, the man said.
But the bird grew still more beautiful.
– I've killed you! the man exclaimed.
He saw the beautiful!

The Sea's Prayer

Tenderly stroking the shore
the sea begged for freedom.

Its breath booming and choking
on the spume of its own spite
the sea was trying to shift, shift the shore.

And again
stroking the shore
the sea solicited.

The shore had been dead
thousands of years.

●

The sun smashed itself into millions of tiny particles and in a
shower of sparks fell to the earth.
The world sank into night.
People struggled for fragments of the light.
I hid a tiny particle of the sun in my heart.
I am warm.

The Invisible Man

I was half dozing, half doodling at my desk when suddenly
there was a crash behind my back.
It was the body of a man.
In its pockets were found the following strange
writings.
. . .

Of course it is amusing when you are invisible and can
do as you please.
But . . .
I have a mother and father. I don't know if mother
ever gave birth to me or not, but I
have a mother.
And now I can see her. She is reading aloud:
– At the feast of the Annunciation, over a little grave
– The white priests sang a psalm
– With a smile the white priests were burying
– A little girl in a blue dress.
I can see her lower lip trembling.
But . . .
To them I am invisible.

You will immediately start imagining what you would have
done in my place. I do it. But . . . I am quite
invisible, you can't even see what I do.

I remember the day distinctly.
Up till that day it had somehow escaped my notice
that a man not only sees and hears people, but people
see and hear him too.
And suddenly (that same morning) I woke with a terrible
foreboding.
The next moment a terrible, inhuman cry burst from
my throat.

Mother was typing.
I went up and put my arm round her shoulders: she carried
on typing. I started to strike the typewriter keys.
Creeping from beneath my strokes I saw:
    – MA-MA, MA-MA, MA-MA, MA-MA

On the white paper I saw, saw these bold letters!
  Mother carried on typing.

All his life my father has written stories about
'how vile, how disgusting man is'.
   He loves only 'posthumously posthumous people'. To
him they are 'a heap of miseries', to him they are
'rubber balls with brushed-up buttons for eyes, with
sheets of corrugated iron for foreheads'.
To him they are 'scraps of meat half chewed by god'.
   BUT I LOVE PEOPLE!
   I kiss the hands of the prostitute about to sell herself.
I tell her how wonderful she is! I tell her
how I love her! She doesn't even have to snatch her hand
away: she just doesn't see me, hear me, feel me.

   I want to do good to people. But what's the point,
if they recognise neither good nor evil anyway.
   If I don't exist!!!

Ivan Kharabarov

●

There's something uneasy in
The air this June midnight.
And beyond the railway's din
I hear cries of pain and fright.

There's something dead in the gaze
Of the joyful, rustling tree.
The whole world's lost in a maze
Of anguished obscurity.

No one knows what's to come
The answer's not to be found.
All breathes and smells of a storm
But there are no clouds, no wind.

●

Down by the Volga fens we strolled
Over the wide land that July
Along the bank, across the field
Nonchalantly, my friend and I.
. . .
And from the river of a sudden
Behind the haystacks' darkening bulk
A woman whom the mist had hidden
Came with a bucket of warm milk.
Sweet with the freshness of new hay
Her kindly fingers from our shirts
Flicked all the dust and grime away
Fastened the collars of our coats.
Russia, it seemed to us, was meant
To be this woman and not she
Who seeks a travel document
And proof of one's identity . . .

Vladimir Kovshin

●

To go where all is bloom
With rowans inaudible
Where a dawn bright with doom
Kindles a barn's straw gable!

Pink castle blossoming
In thatches where doves play!
– And a bat with its wing
Has signalled
The last day.

●

Why are the columns round
So desperately shy
Hiding the corners of
Their crystal grilles? Who thus

Bevelled them, breaking off
Corners and surfaces?
What thought did he intend
For the bird flying by?

●

I heard no clinking coin
I caught a fretful star
And through that light from far
I saw a strange design.

And men weighed down with sorrows
Cried suddenly in chorus
And a new voice resounded.
The awful circle ended.

●

You and I are almost cripples
you and I are almost friends.
Muddy streams have icy ripples:
quickly that temptation ends.

You and I are almost children:
still they lead us by the nose.
Give us something? No, not those.

I myself am far from bold –
wander still through day's nightmare
in this desert white and cold:
wandering hurts more and more.

I seek someone who will tighten
(shyly, tenderly) my strings
and the next time there's a fight on
stay my fist before it swings.

No, no, that way madness lies . . .
I will not cry out for blood.
I have heard a shroud advise:
'Silence is the better road.'

●

Trinity Sunday. Pealing bells
echo across the drizzling rain.
An aged woman wanly smiles
watching the pigeons peck her grain.

And stamping prayers into the crush
like a cross in spun gold inlaid
the good priest's open features flash
through candle points that wink and fade.

And Trinity, and rain, and gold
Russia and God, heads lost in smoke
and (what the guidebooks leave untold)
the prattle of a farmyard cock

the brow, the candles and the prayer
the multitude that swoons and steams
all is so novel and so clear:
Russia and Moloch and the prayer
Russia, the candles and the dreams.

●

to Marina Ivanovna Tsvetayeva

This odour is death, soft and wet
the squalor of rooms with no latch.
It is time to start counting the catch
and busy ourselves with the net.

We are fishermen. None of us grieves:
We drink and drink – that is all
and sing songs that appal
and pay for the songs with our lives.

●

Ulysses returned,
full of space and time
O. E. Mandel'shtam

And space and time
in a blurred grief are welded.
Ulysses smiled
beside a settled war.
And the heavy waves
surged and plunged down
and the ship rolled
and rolled the heavy sea.

But when strange meetings
twisted into bloom
at each rock
at every
changeling shrub
he pitied the paths
and so sadly the canvas swung
when the redhaired mariner
lowered, lowered the sails.

Ulysses, Ulysses
how from a forgotten Ithaca
from all the gentle Eurycleias
through the noise, the glare
the rebukes heaped on your shoulders
you longed that evening
to swing away
sail-like
into the spaces of familiar seas.

Aleksandr Kushner

In the Telegraph Office

In there the mood is sad.
Cables are handy, but
The words 'alive' and 'dead'
Are charged at equal rate.

In there they teach you style.
No needless word, no comma.
How often at the grille
We've caught a whiff of glamour!

Who's last? I'm after you.
Not far away we've pined
With five words tried and true
Poised on an outstretched hand.

The cable-girl surveys –
Stern, without favourite.
When pain confronts her gaze
How does she cope with it?

M. Mertsalov

●

The people of Africa are black people.
They say: you need black happiness.

The people of Asia are yellow people.
They know: yellow happiness is better.

The people of America are white people.
They think: there can only be white happiness.

The people of Russia are Russian people.
They are silent. This is Russian happiness.

●

Words, words – a fine and faceless sum
Minted as civic zeals require:
For me these words have lost their fear
I too have dearly paid for them.

Words, words – where is the standard of these words?
Whence comes my right to write poems and truth?
For them men suffered torture, death.
For them
For a handful of clinking words
For some outline, some tint, some smell
Men let their lives be smashed to shards
Drained their hearts dry in jail and cell.

Words, words – agape and grim
The cellars of Lubyanka lour.
For me these words have lost their fear
I too have dearly paid for them.

Lubyanka : the notorious Moscow prison

Arkady Mikhailov

My Granny is a Witch

I'm a very small boy
& my granny is a witch
I love my granny very much
but she's a witch.
Once on a summer night
she got up and went into the kitchen
I crept after her
& there was a strong smell of onions
up hopped granny on to the frying-pan
and burst out singing ever so loud
& I was ever so frightened
she beckoned to me
and together we flew out of the window
I held on as hard as I could
because the earth below was like a cup
peacocks were strutting over it
and swans swam all in white
it glittered like a Christmas tree
and we dropped into a cake shop
Granny stole some tarts
& I ate them
& Granny ate even more
because she was very tired
& then we came back on a pony
we got undressed ever so quietly
and slipped into bed
Granny told me not to make a noise.
Granny's very kind
it's a pity she's a witch though.

Artyomy Mikhailov

Sphinxes I

●

If you've never been in a concentration camp
If you've never been tortured
If your best friend has never denounced you
And you've never crawled out of a heap of corpses
After surviving execution by a miracle
If you don't know the theory of relativity
And tensor calculus
If you can't do a ton on a motorbike
If you've never killed the girl you love on orders from
     outside
If you can't build transistor radios
If you've never been in any kind of mafia
And can't forget yourself and shout 'Hurray' with the others
If you can't hide from an atomic blast in two seconds
If you can't dress at the expense of food
If five of you can't live in five square metres
And don't even play basketball
– Man, the 20th century's not for you!

N. Nor

Phoenix 1

To My Friends

No, ours is not to fire a volley
Into the capped and booted throng!
For poets there is no such folly
Before an enemy so strong.
No, no Revolt shall thrill our ears
Reborn in us that fateful hour!
For our concern is with ideas
And not for us the rod of power.
No, ours is not to shoot – we know it!
But in response to real alarms
The period creates the poet
And he creates the man-at-arms.

If suddenly you come for me
To throw me in an iron cage
I'll leave the world with head held high
And I shall not repent or rage.
I'll step into the cold abyss
With no appeals, complaints or tears:
Nor shall my Vision be amiss –
Her I have cherished down the years.
And far from friends, between thick walls
We'll live to see the day we're free.
I do not fear your long-term jails.
She dies not, nor can you kill me.

1959

We shall not go down Broadway or the Strand
Or make safaris in the wilderness.
Our knowledge comes from never-never land
We build our world from gossip and the press.

Bulat Okujava

Johnny Morozov

Don't blame it on Johnny Morozov –
you see, it's not really his fault.
That girl turned his head, bit his nose off –
poor him, it's not really his fault.

He went to the circus in Norwood
and fell for a girl in the ring.
He might have found someone straightforward
but no, it was her in the ring.

With only a few of her clothes off
she walked up the tightrope and waved
and passion possessed poor Morozov
with horny hand held him enslaved.

He threw away hundreds of roubles
(to him it was all much the same).
His girl pined away full of troubles –
to her it was not all the same.

He started to dine on medusa
to keep this new bird satisfied.
He offered (indeed) to seduce her –
just so she'd feel happy inside.

He didn't see mischief was brewing
all thanks to that circus-ring sylph.
Oh Johnny! Oh what are you doing!
You're up on the tightrope yourself.

The Paper Soldier

Now once there was a soldier boy
Handsome and bold as bold can be
But he was just a children's toy:
He was a paper soldier, see.

He wanted to remake the world
For all men to live happily
But round the bedpost he was twirled:
He was a paper soldier, see.

Ready amid the fire and smoke
Twice over he'd lie doun and dee.
You looked upon him as a joke:
He was a paper soldier, see.

You didn't think he could be trusted
With things demanding secrecy.
And why? in case you're interested
He was a paper soldier, see.

But he would fret and curse his lot
Long for a life that's wild and free.
Fire! Fire! he begged. He quite forgot
He was a paper soldier, see.

Fire? Very well.
Here: come along!
And off into the fire went he
And burnt to cinders for a song.
He was a paper soldier, see.

The Black Cat

Round the back way there is a gate
that bears the sign NO HAWKERS:
here lives – the lord of his estate –
a cat as black as Orcus.

Beneath his whiskers lurks a grin
the darkness is his shield.
While other cats make all the din
the black cat's lips are sealed.

Rats? Mice? He's lost his taste for both –
he just sits in the passage
and catches us upon our oath
upon a bit of sausage.

He doesn't hunt or beg for game
his yellow eye glows roundly:
we all bring offerings to him
and then say 'thank you kindly'.

He doesn't make a single noise
he only drinks and eats
and when he's sharpening his claws
it might be on our throats.

That's why our house is in poor shape
and life is far from funny . . .
We ought to hang a lantern up –
but we can't raise the money.

A poem about Stalin

●

All night the cocks were crowing
and their bright eyes were shutting
and back their heads were throwing
as if they were reciting.
But something in their throttles
recalled the caustic sorrow
of shamefaced men in brothels
tomorrow and tomorrow.
The cry was drained of feeling
and fell as wide and nerveless
as looking at the ceiling
they stroke the strange and loveless
when they are well past caring
and yet cannot say no.

All night the dark was staring
and all night would not go.

Song About Fools

So nowadays it is the rule –
for every ebb there is a flow
for every wise man there's a fool
and everything works out just so.

But fools find this arrangement galls –
from all sides you can see right through them.
People shout at the fools 'Fools! Fools!'
and this is very hurtful to them.

So to make fools less noticeable
and everybody still more equal
to wise men was affixed a label
to guarantee a happy sequel.

The label system never fails –
a poundsworth for a copper farthing.
People shout at the wise 'Fools! Fools!'
and this way all the fools are laughing.

●

I'll get me cap and jacket
me kitbag and I'll pack it
and chuck it on me shoulder:
it's great to be a soldier.

Life's all by easy stages –
no need for work or wages.
I'll swing it like I told yer:
it's great to be a soldier.

And if you get the order
there's no such thing as murder.
Guilty? – but they can't hold yer:
you're just a simple soldier.

This poem was once known as 'Song of the American Soldier'

Song About the Drummer

Get up at the dawn's first glimmer
when the milkman's on his rounds
and you'll see the happy drummer
with his drumsticks in his hands.

Midday comes with reeking clamour
clanging trams and tramping feet:
hark – you'll hear the happy drummer
marching, marching down the street.

Then with all its shady glamour
comes the evening, conman, cheat:
look – you'll see the happy drummer
marching, marching down the street.

The drum beat – now sharp, now dimmer
through the clamour, darkness, sleet:
can't you hear the happy drummer
marching, marching down the street?

How sad you can't hear the drummer
marching, marching down the street.

A. Onyezhskaya

Phoenix 1

Moscow Gold

Golden the jabbing pains
In the black dark of hell
Golden the thoughts in chains
Golden the folk in jail.
Wealth everywhere: gold bread
Gold braid around the banner
And in the gold cowshed
The golden roll of honour
Of those who glorified
This city, land and world
Among them, glowing with pride
The idol heaped with gold
The latest, brightest name
The people's friend who spills
His golden gifts to cram
The smiles of imbeciles.
Golden the five year plan
And even teeth wear crowns –
Everything's lovely in
My fatherland built on bones.

Lost Joy

Maybe this joy will come
And maybe it will not
Yet for ever are this light
        This gloom
This black sun in the soul.
You don't remember me
I've forgotten you
Dazzled in the dark
We don't see each other –
Earth has long since dispensed
        With lovers and poets.
I know the frail thread will
Break between heart and heart
I shall break off and still
        My cry
Someone gentle and grey will come
To wind this world in a web.

Listen, drops fall –
Rain or tears?
Mankind weeps
With dry eyes
And fates and men
Weave ropes, not songs . . .
The souls of the dead are ashamed of the living
Maybe this joy
Has dissolved like a puff of stream
Maybe like a beggar it
            Stands at the gate.
A bronze bell strikes
Heart opens, memory
Stands guard over elements
Heart has buried.
The world shoots poets
Puts them in a common grave
Sets a cross on free songs –
On poets no crosses stand
Dazzled
In the gloom millions live
Who have heard no songs
But the song from the knout
Or from beneath the knout.

To My Generation

Snow scatters where your foot treads
Laughter peals like dainty bells . . .
Why do you kneel to old gods?
Why do you chalk prayers on walls?
Why do you bow down to earth?
Why look out for heaven's treasure?
Have you dreamed of spring's rebirth
Or have you grown weak from pleasure?!
Why crush flowers beneath your heel?
Why count out the grains of corn?
Either you are clear of evil! . . .
Or has your heart turned to stone?
Snow scatters where your foot treads

From heaven falls the spring rain.
Why do you kneel to strange gods
And reap where you have not sown?
Laughter peals like dainty bells
Brave folk dream of spring's rebirth:
Where is your bronze bell that thrills –
The fulcrum that moves the earth?

Yury Pankratov

Slow Song

The ship goes off into the sea
The ship goes off into the sea
The ship goes off into the sea
Far, so far.

The sea goes off into the sky
The sea goes off into the sky
The sea goes off into the sky
High, so high.

The sky goes away to the stars
The sky goes away to the stars
The sky goes away to the stars
Green and blue.

The stars go off into eternity
The stars go off into eternity
The stars go off into eternity
All the time.

Eternity goes off to men
Eternity comes off to men
Eternity comes down to men
Great and small.

And men go off into the sea
And men go off into the sea
And men go off into the sea
And men go . . .

Muza Pavlova

●

Painter, draw me a friend
with boyish shoulders
unhurried lean arms
and long, unRussian fingers
and a reluctant neck
an adam's apple emphasised by the collar
making him look like a man
and a noble chin
and a mouth as though painted on
fleshy
exaggerated and red like a clown's
and a proud, birdlike nose
and beneath a thatch of unruly hair
eyes
still full
of terror in the face of life.

Herman Plisetsky

The Pipe

The Circus lions roared.
In Floral Street
the flowers inclined towards the morning market.
None of us gave a thought to the Nyeglinka –
the unseen stream, the slinker under concrete.
The thoughts of everybody were elsewhere:
flower life is all surface like a sphere
a fabulous balloon at bursting point . . .
While down below the river blindly gropes
and the mist seeps and drips from shaft and vent.

When on the city pour torrential rains
Nyeglinka flings the covers off the drains.
When in the Kremlin eminences die
the floodtide of the people rises high . . .
From Plummet Square and Presentation Gate
the folk came rolling in a headlong stream
an avalanche along the wide black street.
The Pipe, the Pipe – a whirlpool thick as night
surmounted by a canopy of steam!
Pipe, Waterpipe, for twelve years till today
you have been trickling from me down the drain
your lawns have grown the daisies of routine
you've wanted to be bygone, not to matter
forgotten in the tramway's cheerful clatter.
Pipe, Waterpipe, for twelve years till today
you've grown in caves of memory underground
devoid of any movement, any sound –
and you have broken free
gushed from the drains
and you have carried, you have carried me!

A flood has no reflection – only fear
with courage to hold fast and not to fail
standing to lose your hide to save your pride.
The girl who drowned is truth – her feet are bare
she appals, she is so wretched and so frail.
Beneath the black loudspeakers in the morning
with eyes black edged through loss of sleep and yawning
fathers take up their stance
in underpants . . .

The commentator spreads forth his black crape —
the unseen voice, so firm and reassuring
that in precisely the same tone proclaims
the State's will, names the heroes
and condemns . . .
Today he flies at half mast — hear him droop:
God has a lot of sugar in his urine!

March makes the morning keen and watery eyed.
Licking away leftover scraps of snow
to puddles in the street the shed tears flow.
Along the streets, oblivious of the puddles
flowing to where they teach and work come huddles
of blind somnambulists from every side.
Against the city sky in bright relief
gigantic festive portraits bob and hang:
the universal hymn, so long unsung
stirs souls into an ecstasy of grief.

Into this walking, wandering Moscow I
melt, I lose individuality
I lose depth, I become a cardboard shape:
faceless and like a wave the element
surges to overwhelm me and to sweep
away the cordons of militiamen!
And as a dot I flow into the stream
on to the pavements rushing with the tide
a ground swell pounding the dark firmament
above the city where the god has died
where vehicles are flat upon their backs
and trolleybuses have had heart attacks
and paralysed are parallel tram tracks . . .
And somewhere
in the middle of it all
deep in the very heart smokes this black hole . . .
Oh, feel an elbow
hard against your ribs!
Thronging all round you are the champions
of all ranks, age groups and trade unions . . .
Out there, in front, between the granite blocks
like breakwaters to check a river's flow
the lorries have been set out in a row.

This column is of iron, inanimate:
the only words it knows are 'stop' and 'halt'.
The howling avalanche it strives to force
into its channel
churn into its course:
inflexible, it has the power to press
and mince the monstrous babbling sobbing mass.

Out there, in front, amid the river's rage
a vulgar *Illustrated* colour page
it might be – in a red and gilded pall
rises the vision of the mourning hall.
There the sarcophagus with the exalted
little old man inside is standing tilted
to show this is no ordinary corpse:
exalted even now by drums and pipes
above the walls, the mob of weeping men –
assisted by Chopin and Beethoven.

Onward, and ever onward, freemen slaves
trampled by tsardoms into glorious graves!
Out there, in front, there's no way through the crush –
choke!
Gape and gulp with mouths like little fish!
Onward, onward, makers of history!
The roadway cobbles shall be your reward
the crunching of your ribs
the wrought iron railing
the roaring thunder of the maddened herd
and bloodless lips tidemarked with blood and mud:
no drums or pipes shall sound at your souls' sailing!
You shall be squeezed and flattened on all sides
must make do with a heaven drained of gods
a godless heaven trimmed with ragged clouds
make do with this black sky when you are dead
as when alive you made do with black bread.
Your eye socket, clean to the very bone
shall testify to you that truth is black
that Earth amid the blackness of the sky
is utterly alone.
And all its flowers

its brilliant blue dome, its airy towers
are florid fancy
that the Pipe devours.
All of Earth's oxygen is burnt and lost
inside this cauldron's seething holocaust . . .

Let's pull ourselves together –
try to save
the barefoot girl who fell beneath our wave!
And in a mob of less than men let's dare
to be plain people
whom once love begot!
Let's give up hope, and wearily retire
to dry our tattered trousers by the fire
to drink a glass
sit up and fathom out
how to breathe in a city with no air . . .

Pipe, Waterpipe!
You in the Day of Wrath
will summon all the dead to gather here
will summon those transparent little girls
stamped out by madness with its white eyed stare
will summon those who blackened at the mouth
delivered from the doorways to the morgue
and resurrected by the Doom Pipe's blare . . .

My five foot iamb, born before the Flood
plod on
past every manhole, every drain.
Put up your collar, cover up your face
shut yourself in, enclosed like the Ring Road –
the Garden
that for thirty years has been
the course of the time-honoured relay race.
Bubble in the mist, you subterranean stream
froth in the gloom, giving off clouds of steam:
we keep forgetting you are there, and then
flower life blossoms on the movie screen
and oxygen in plenty swells the chest:
driven for ever downward you exist

deep in my iron-
saturated blood . . .

Onward and onward!
There is no way back!
The drain is sealed, there is no overflow!

And this is all that we shall ever know.

1965

The reference is to the stampede in Moscow's Trubnaya Square
during Stalin's lying-in-state (recounted by Yevtushenko in his
Precocious Autobiography)

L. Ryzhova

Psalm 137

By Babylon's sad streams
There we sat down and wept
Recalling Zion's psalms
In the black midnight's depth.

We hung our harps aloft
There in the willow grove
And desert children scoffed:
Sing songs of holy love!

How can we, bound together
With tears and bars of iron?
Tongue, perish! Right hand, wither!
If we lose sight of Zion.

As though alive, too lovely
Is our throne, smashed by fools.
Remember, Lord, the ungodly
Who sacked her holy jewels.

Daughter of Babylon!
How blest who calls you whore
And hurls your kin and coin
Against the granite shore.

Psalm 137: Orthodox (and Vulgate) Psalm 136

Henrikh Sabgir

Icarus

A sculptor
Moulded Icarus.
The model went back
Muttering 'The hack –
I've got a heart
Not an engine part.'
Friends came.
'Trite!' they said. 'Tedious!'
Only women acclaim
This work of genius.
'How moving!'
'Things are improving!'
'Tradition . . .
Ancient Grecian . . .'
'Sexual emotion . . .'
'I want babies
By a gearbox!'
She conceived – and in gear
In top gear
With a roar
She bore
A helicopter.
It flies and cries
Calls to its mother.
There it goes, up into the sky
Breaking each onlooker's heart.
SUCH IS THE EDUCATIONAL
      INFLUENCE OF ART.
The artist took his bow.
There's a bust in the square now:
A self-portrait –
Dustcart
Telephone
Slot-machine.

David Samoilov

●

Do not trust the disciples. They will betray the cause
They will break it apart, will take it, will make off with it
They will dishonour the spirit, they will bury the body
They will not suffer the bones to moulder at rest in the clay.

Do not trust the disciples. Put them from you in peace.
Cast their staves out behind them, and relinquish your
   calling.
Then, King Jesus, revolt! Send the evangelists packing!
And to Golgotha wend your steep and solitary way.

A. Shchukin

People, Listen!

People, listen!
People, listen!
This is me calling you.

People, listen!
Moscow calling.
Moscow calling.

Spasskaya tower
Bongs out the hour
And the dark Square
Stands huge and bare
Stands Red
The Square in the gloom
With the red name
The Square called Red.

I used to think
Well where's the paint?
I used to think
Well where's the blood?
Boot blacking
I used to think
Rubbed the paint off
Trod the blood in.
There is no paint!
There is no blood!
Don't listen, people!
Don't listen, people!
The Square wears a mask –
Boot blacking
The Almighty's caress
The general whacking.
We're the most fullblooded
We're the most redblooded
So sing us your dirges
So bring us your purges!
The tsars may have spilled us
But they haven't killed us.
Into the hoary old Kremlin we crawled

And issued a decree for all the world.
We marked out our borders
And barked out our orders.
We built our houses
And held carouses.
We started to tell
New tales
We started to sing
New songs.

But everything stayed
The way it was.
So what, that men are fed
And shod?
Where they are not
It's goodbye to rules
Or else you've got
A land of fools.

. . .

Enough! That'll do!
Comrades in the Soviets
Remember the days of '17
Forgotten, eh?
Today
The sixties are thick
With poets in Russia!

. . .

Red Square sleeps
Snow has fallen
The first snow
People slumber
Red Square sleeps
A shot rings out –
One man
Any number . . .
Red Square sleeps
Snow has fallen
The first snow
But people

Slumber.
Wake them up, maybe?
– Look, listen!
Snow has fallen and a man . . .
People, listen!
People, listen!
– No, no, no.

You don't want to. I know.
You're sick of it. I know.
– Enough! That'll do!
– Shut up, you!
You don't want to, I know.
You're sick of it. I know.
You mustn't. Understand?
Or else you too . . .

Red Square sleeps
Snow has fallen
People slumber, slumber.

Snow it is red
In Russia the red
On the Square called Red
Snow has fallen red
And people see, not sleep.

I used to think
Well where's the paint?
I used to think
Well where's the blood?

Boot blacking
I used to think
Rubbed the paint off
Trod the blood in.

People, listen!
People, listen!
Now understand
It all to the end.

People, listen!
People, listen!
Moscow calling.
Moscow calling.

The Hothouse

The hothouse, December.
Orchid bloom, on the walls mould.
And the air acrid –
A tinny smell
Quick! Quick!
Don't dare to look –
In the hothouse
There's a font.
And in a row
The spendthrifts grow –
Puffed out with fat
Their bloom a dried fig.
They wait for the end –
The narcissus sighs.
They hover for blood –
The narcissus dies.

Surely even
The roses blushed
In the hothouse
In the hothouse
Surely the gossip –
The simple
Daisy
What brought her here
The likes of her?
Surely too
Surely tears
And the mimosa
Flower is frozen.

But instead the roses
Bloom and fatten
In the hothouse
In the hothouse
Ever reddening
And not blushing
Roses in bed
Roses in April
Roses getting fat
Roses getting rude
In the hothouse
In the hothouse!

In the hothouse:
– No need for the red
No need for the white
No need for the varied
In hothouses.
We want the grey
And the blue
        On dark blue twigs
        Forgetting it all
We want to listen
To orchid bloom.
THE HOTHOUSE! –
For the upstarts
For the cashers-in
For the hawkers
Of roses and gourds
Of lives and words.
The hothouse – I can't take it!
I've no regrets, black nights
Candles black
Orchid bloom
I shan't make it, red rose
Remember those tears, those
Years ago!

Leonid Shkol'nik

The Lads

Pingpong
       thoughts
Will hop
       like bobtailed flies –
We're the egghead lads
Of no revolution.
We've knocked conscience
               unconscious
Beatified
       with bolts and bars
We walk
       through pineweeds
In the dark
       like owls.
We look for horizons in hovels
We forage for the
         buzz
            of rustling
In the fumbling of the
           man who grovels
In prophets' promises
Where the joy
       of their
          truth
Is in store
      for us too
And where ponies
        are shod
With clover.

The Trojan Horse

Thinkers
      put on your thinkingcaps
            and think.
Remember
      past remembrances
and those whose thoughts spy out the atom
                mumbling
in knotted labyrinthine groves.

Remember
        as you fill your
brains with the
burning
chill of
chiming
stars
    striking a midnight
shod with the crooked
crutches of the depraved and
              deprived.
We who are
        beaten off by reflections in windows
        from a strident
              red trap
we who are written off can only howl –
hugging yellow reveries
between our shattered elbows.
We drowned in drumming Tartar hoofs
and then fire, fire, fire.
For seven centuries
        we've held on
           we've hung on
WHERE ARE YOU, TROJAN HORSE?
Why don't you
over the black asphalt
         all a-holler
over the brow of the planned
          kingdom

leap?
WE'RE
STILL ALIVE.

Boris Slutsky

Sphinxes 1

●

Fears, jeers, tears
And all that caper
Aren't worth the ink
Aren't worth the paper.
Blots and smears
Aren't worth the ink
Nor what gives off
A moral stink.
Go and write odes
Where 'liberty'
Lamely rhymes
With 'brotherly'.
Go and write ballads
Where words like 'dinner'
Rhyme perfectly
With words like 'winner'.
Your talents
I will always heed
And your ballads
Will always read.

●

In the state there is the law
Citizens cannot ignore.
In the anti-state the sheep
Have a private rule they keep.

Under rule of law the folk
Serve what gives them food and drink
But rebellion has no book
And revolt no pen and ink.

When rebellion goes to press
When revolt takes up a pen
It has donned official dress
Nourishes the sons of men

Codifies its rights and wrongs
Rids the aged of their qualms.
Revolutionary songs
Are replaced by hymns and psalms.

Yury Stefanov

from The Descent Into Hell

Aghast, for vodka
and lard that bought her
the homeland danced
like Herod's daughter.

All lost for the
foul deed, foul wish
a thousand heads
lie on the dish.

Here – O my people
use your eyes! –
a millennium
of glory lies.

A hydra
of miracles we have:
the red dish
is Svyatoslav

the dish of storms
is Feofan
the fog-dish
Rublyov, holy man.

Nikon and archpriest
Avvakum
terrible, wild
stare through the gloom

from blocks and boards
where the blood runs.
The bells
ring for the ruined ones.

My people, hear
the death knell ring:
to Herod
Russia sold her King.

. . .

O Lord God
listen to my prayer!
I know – it is
one grief we share:

grant me
with Russia to descend
into the darkness
underground.

Down slippery steps
with soft footfall
to Russia in Hades
to Russia in hell

I will shyly come
and gently call:
To you my body
and blood and soul!

I will bow to you:
the blood, the slough
with my lifeblood
Russia, wash off

and in two pieces
tear my flesh
and with its cloth
your face refresh.

In strength and glory
shine, excel.

For Russia I
will remain in hell!

1963

Poetry

Sun of blood and stars of sorrow
The cold milky way of mind
Are like oxen's necks unspanned
Yet by yoke. A holy, terrible

> Yoke must jam together star
> Sun and milky way before
> Your pen's plough on the white arable
> Can engrave the first line's furrow.

●

Russia, your image
Doubles in my soul:
Are you song or howl?
Are you bird or bitch?

> Will your steppes' grasses
> Bark of your forests
> Like a beast's withers
> Or halcyon's feathers
> Rise up before me
> On the final day?

> > Are you song or howl?
> > Deathlessness, decay?

halcyon: Russian *alkonost*, mythical bird with human face,
apparently akin to the halcyon

Aleksandr Timofeyevsky

The Word

The word has been debased as a worn coin
But now I want to raise it up again!
For all to see the brilliance of the metal
Surely a life's devotion is too little!
Naked as truth the word first saw the day:
It fluttered like a pigeon in the sky
And for it men went out to starve and die.
In the heartbeat its thunder would resound
Until it fell into the murderer's hand.
Where the thief worked with mailed fist and with knout
The word's own marks and features found it out.
Over his stranglehold it set a hood
And hid behind a mask of mud and blood
And the thief sent a lie across the world
In words whose sense had been twisted and curled.
Hypocrites put it in a publication
That reached a multi-million circulation.
The word was prostituted in rich houses
In radio programmes full of empty noises
It was reiterated unctuously
On working days and days of jubilee.
The word was getting fat, began to swell
Bedevilled everybody . . . and it fell.
The word has been debased as a worn coin.
Who if not we
                    must raise it up again?

●

Nausea has me in its grip
The gripes attack me and I vomit.
I know – the fight is without hope
But there is no escaping from it.
About my shoulders darkness falls
Leers out of windows that are blind
To torture me with caterwauls
And flaunt the muteness of mankind.
Then blackness ties me to its rack
Slinks to my throat like a vampire
And all the house is filled with smoke

And stench from my frayed nerves on fire.
I want to wake – not just the street
But the whole planet from its yawn
But the moon's rusty old tin plate
Commands my silence till the dawn
Tells me to lie and try to sleep
Testing my terror to the limit.
Nausea has me in its grip
And there is no escaping from it.

It shrills, shrills through the heart, and then it
Will be scourged when the day has beckoned
With the whips of each weighted minute
And the thin lashes of each second.

Vladimir Uflyand

After a Symphony Concert

I have not had my mental image fixed
to understand a tune without a text.

How do I tell with no word-base if it
is hostile
or Soviet?

Song
is where I belong:
text and tune.
By 'Fatherland' this is some of what we mean.
Like sunshine, highway, home.
In music too it is the chiefest form.

O had I but two good songs up my sleeve
I'd be a singer by now.
But that's impossible to realise
if
they try to write nothing but symphonies.

Aleksandr Vasyutkov

from The Tale of Bogolyubovo

Introduction

The little bluebells
Nod to and fro.
Above their heads
The grass does not grow.
Crowding the road
To the village they come.
So in Suzdal', in Suzdal'
The bells, the bells bloom.
The pigeons they marry
Beneath the church roofs
Soon the bellringers
Will wring out their griefs.
In an age super-modern
Our sleep they are breaking
Upon our closed eyelids
The bells they are striking.

Chapter I

Bells!
      Bells over Suzdal'!
                  Over Bogolyubovo!
The paunches of stupid
              boyars are rocking!
And brocades, sables –
              on every side.
And down from cathedrals
                  black ravens glide.

*'. . . And having taken command of the land of Suzdal',
Andrei did banish his father's old boyars, his father's
chief men . . .'*
                  (from Russian history)

A new prince on the throne –
                 a cask of vodka on the table.
'Glory! Glory
         to Andrei
                Bogolyubsky!'

Sandals clattered
The dance began.
By Andrei's palace
Lurched drunken men.
Hands grab at skirts
Of warm, unkissed wenches.
Apprentice church-workers
Slump beneath benches.
Holding a stick like a fiddler's bow
A peasant is crooning soft and low:
'In Russia the White
The princes would bite
Like dull, gilded fish
                to honour your dish.
Oh, wide of the mark
                in Russia the dark!'
But the new boyars
Those sullen defiers
Their black beards caress
                  cast glances around
Red gobs puff and hiss
                  but no other sound.
While nimble non-Russians
Grow fat on the feast
And loud conversations
Rise bubbling like yeast.
Russian and foreigner
                here eat their fill.
The prince to the aliens offers goodwill:
'O Hannibal, Hannibal
                pour out the wine
Pour out the wine
              for the bountiful prince
Have I not given thee comfort and room
O wandering savage that knewest no home . . .'
Till daybreak the torches flickered.
Roasting and spice were rank.
At first light the sun wept over
The village stretched out dead drunk.

. . . the prince continues stern with his new boyars.
A plot is hatched. On 29th June 1174, Andrei Bogolyubsky
was murdered. Three omitted chapters give the reason
for the murder and details of the prince's death.
  And now, the morning after the murder . . .

Chapter 5

All through the town the cudgels strolled.
The boyars' sons were running wild.
'We're not old Andrei, we're from the north.
Come shovel out your silver and gold!'
. . . The gilded domes of churches
Had blackened and gone bald . . .
The people cried, the horses shied
Around a weeping willow.
And in the wind like eagles red
Red shirts did flap and billow.
And from above, a hellish blue
Brought passions to the boil:
The strident sky was tottering
But knew not how to fall.
Beneath the reckless axe's gleam
The master builders met their doom.
'Foreigners! beasts in alien rags!
Bastards! O prince's folly . . .'
The blood flowed red from horny hands
In the drunken hurly-burly.
Scrawny shoulders quivered
(For want of something warm).
The rough ropes of the peasants
Cut into each velvet arm.
One cocked his head as though in jest.
He laughed hysterically.
Through rents at his bare shoulderblades
The sweat glittered like beads
And through his finger chinks there flashed
An eye of frenzied lustre.
'Repent! Repent!' they screamed at him
Hurling alabaster.

He bowed and bowed like a clockwork doll
Forgetting shame and pride.
But the church he had left incomplete
Was not to be denied.
She like a swan emerged
Her domes a flaming crown
And throwing aside her veil
Soared far above all evil.
She was keen as a Russian song
Her tune like clear bells sounded.
The young apprentices looked long
Clutching their caps, dumbfounded . . .

Aida Yaskolka

●

In any soul there is a bright
                              country
Where there is peace
                    and coolness
                              in summer's heat
But not for me!
To me all life is war
Peace sets my teeth on edge!
But should it come
                  let trees fall
Flowers wither
              islands drown
And all my lofty words
                      touch
With greatness no one's soul.

Mikhail Yeryomin

●

The cross of antlers, idol-like, the stag
Raises aloft through crowns of thornbushes
The doe he does not win but saws her out
From the most tender muscles of the rival.
The trumpet-horn sounds in the vale
And wounds the side to salt.
The pretty hinds inhale
The cruel smell of father and son.